skipper

practical course notes

Written by: Andy Thompson
Penny Haire
Simon Jinks
Illustrations by: Sarah Selman
Typeset: Creativebyte
Printed in China through World Print Ltd.
Reprinted May 2010

www.rya.org.uk

Royal Yachting Association
RYA House, Ensign Way, Hamble, Southampton SO31 4YA
Tel: 0844 556 9555 Fax: 0844 556 9516
email: training@rya.org.uk website: www.rya.org.uk

British Cataloguing in Publication Date:
A Catalogue record of this book is available from the British Library.
ISBN. 1905104138

CONTENTS

More than 11,000 people, throughout the world, successfully complete a RYA Day Skipper course every year.

The courses are run by over 320 RYA Training Centres around the UK and overseas. Using a RYA recognised centre will ensure that you are taught to the RYA's high standards, and your course will be safe, informative and enjoyable.

Day Skipper Practical Course Notes has been compiled to complement the Day Skipper Practical course and draws on the cumulative experience of hundreds of experienced sailing instructors. The techniques shown or described are tried and tested and are suitable for most types of cruising yacht.

I hope that you enjoy the book and find it useful. Good sailing!

Simon Jinks
RYA Chief Cruising Instructor

Prepare the yacht for sea before leaving harbour. Brief the crew about the passage and consider the crew strengths.

Crew

Give a safety brief.

Brief the crew about the passage.

Check if any crew have a medical condition you should be aware of.

Check lifejackets and harnesses are adjusted correctly.

Advise sea sick prone crew to take medication.

Weather

Obtain the latest weather forecast.

Check the local conditions.

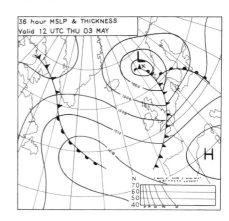

Victualling

Ensure there is enough food and drink.

Prepare meals for a passage in advance.

Stow snacks in readily accessible areas.

Navigation

Prepare a passage and pilotage plan.

Check charts are up to date and give adequate coverage.

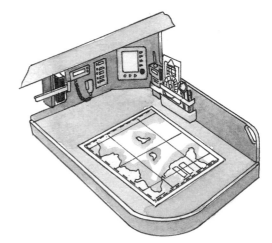

Fuel

- Check there is sufficient fuel.

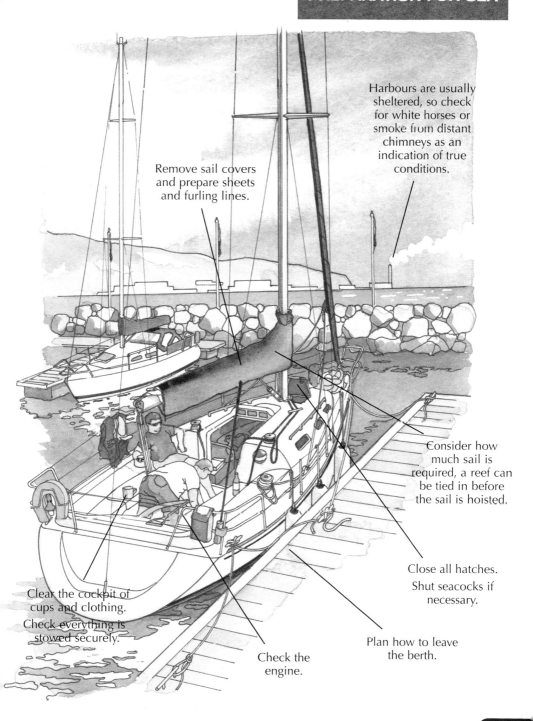

Remove sail covers and prepare sheets and furling lines.

Harbours are usually sheltered, so check for white horses or smoke from distant chimneys as an indication of true conditions.

Consider how much sail is required, a reef can be tied in before the sail is hoisted.

Close all hatches. Shut seacocks if necessary.

Clear the cockpit of cups and clothing. Check everything is stowed securely.

Plan how to leave the berth.

Check the engine.

A daily engine check is the best way to spot potential problems. Engine problems are the most common cause for lifeboat callouts, most are preventable by regular checks.

Use a daily check to look for: oil, fuel or water leaks; loose belts; signs of wear; lube oil levels.

Keep the fuel tank full to avoid condensation and water in the fuel. A low level disturbs sediment in the tank which could block fuel filters.

Top-up levels if required.

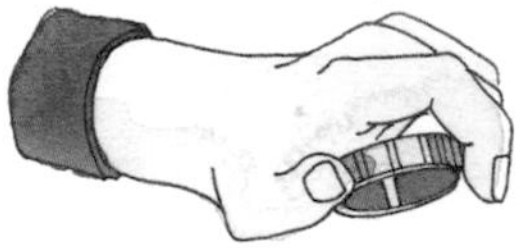

gearbox dipstick

Check the gearbox oil weekly or every 30 hours.

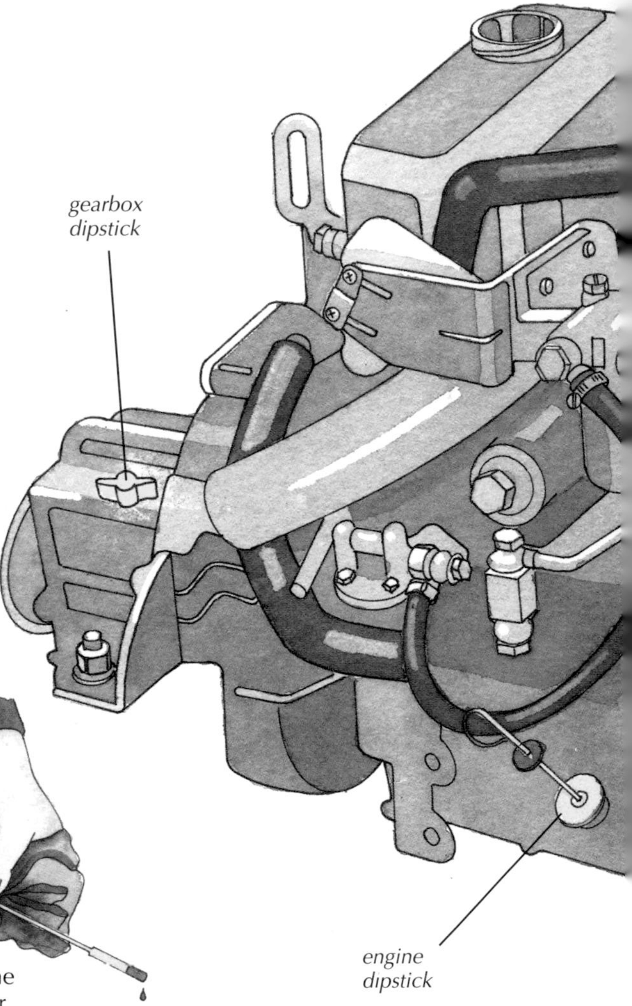

engine dipstick

Check the oil level is between the dipstick markers. A milky colour indicates cooling water and oil are mixing, if so, call an engineer.

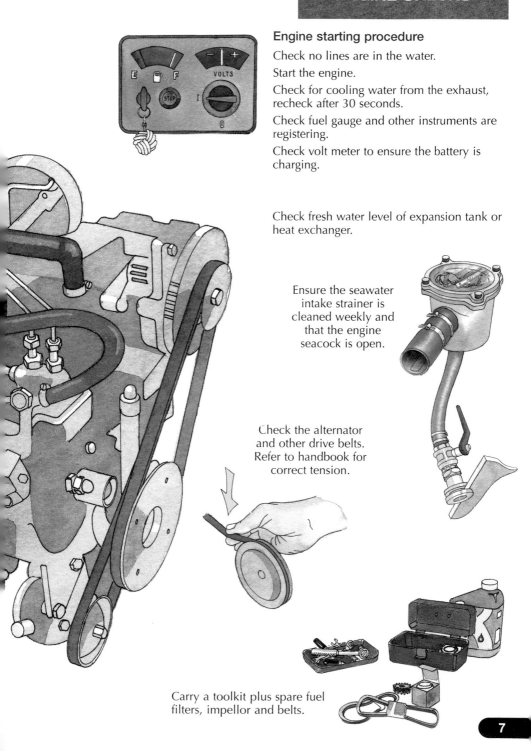

Engine starting procedure

Check no lines are in the water.

Start the engine.

Check for cooling water from the exhaust, recheck after 30 seconds.

Check fuel gauge and other instruments are registering.

Check volt meter to ensure the battery is charging.

Check fresh water level of expansion tank or heat exchanger.

Ensure the seawater intake strainer is cleaned weekly and that the engine seacock is open.

Check the alternator and other drive belts. Refer to handbook for correct tension.

Carry a toolkit plus spare fuel filters, impellor and belts.

Boats are designed to sail upright or heeled up to 20 degrees, this is when they are most comfortable to sail.

If the boat feels uncomfortable, reduce the sail area.

Results of excessive heeling are;

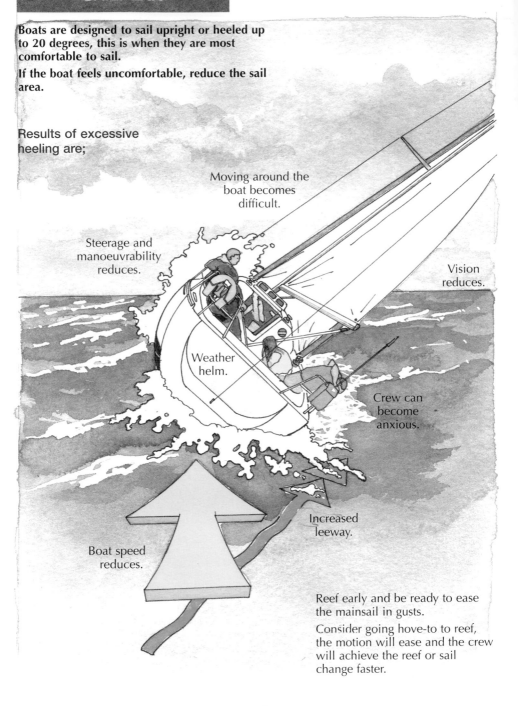

Moving around the boat becomes difficult.

Steerage and manoeuvrability reduces.

Vision reduces.

Weather helm.

Crew can become anxious.

Increased leeway.

Boat speed reduces.

Reef early and be ready to ease the mainsail in gusts.

Consider going hove-to to reef, the motion will ease and the crew will achieve the reef or sail change faster.

Sail selection is a key part of preparing to go to sea. If in doubt, put in a reef and prepare a smaller headsail before you depart. It is always easier to put more sail up than to take it down.

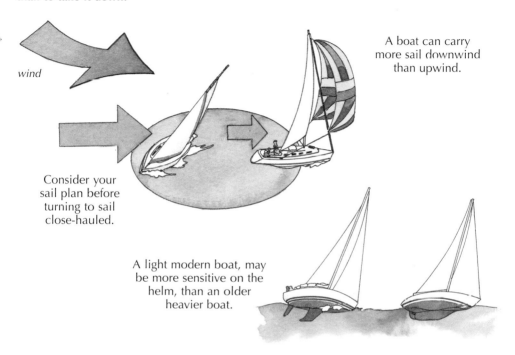

wind

A boat can carry more sail downwind than upwind.

Consider your sail plan before turning to sail close-hauled.

A light modern boat, may be more sensitive on the helm, than an older heavier boat.

For a typical modern boat, these guidelines may help prepare the right amount of sail. Reduce headsail, then mainsail to keep the sail plan balanced.

Wind speed in knots	0-12	13-15	16-20	21-25	26-30	31-35
Main	Full	Full	1 reef	2 reefs	3 reefs	3 reefs
Jib (Headsail)	Full	Full	3/4	1/2	1/3	Storm jib

Give a safety brief covering where the safety equipment is kept, how it works and when to use it.

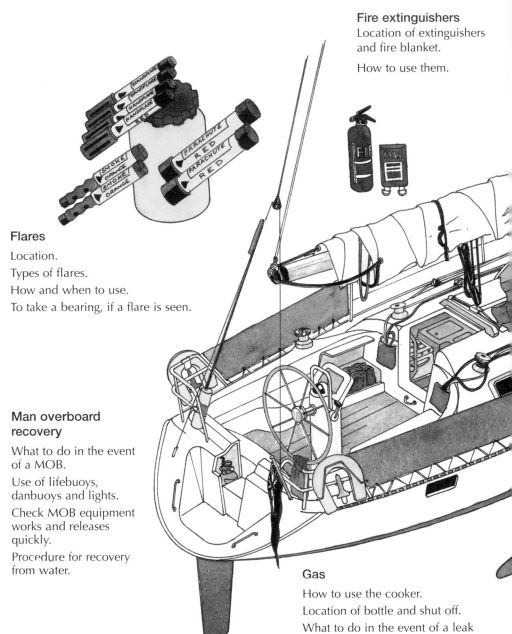

Fire extinguishers

Location of extinguishers and fire blanket.

How to use them.

Flares

Location.

Types of flares.

How and when to use.

To take a bearing, if a flare is seen.

Man overboard recovery

What to do in the event of a MOB.

Use of lifebuoys, danbuoys and lights.

Check MOB equipment works and releases quickly.

Procedure for recovery from water.

Gas

How to use the cooker.

Location of bottle and shut off.

What to do in the event of a leak (ventilate) – no naked flames.

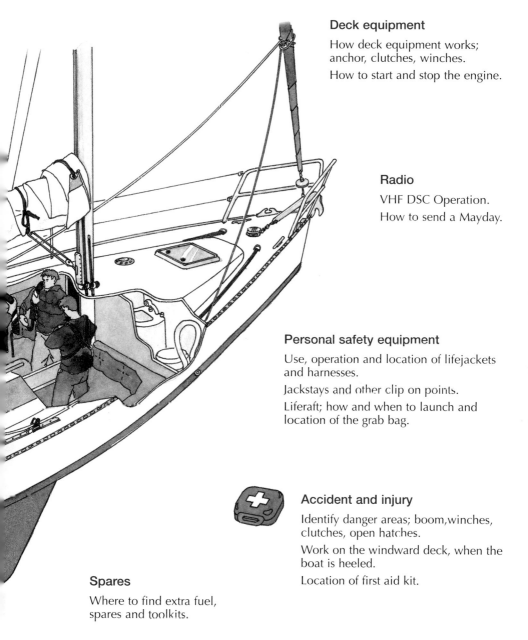

Deck equipment

How deck equipment works;
anchor, clutches, winches.

How to start and stop the engine.

Radio

VHF DSC Operation.

How to send a Mayday.

Personal safety equipment

Use, operation and location of lifejackets
and harnesses.

Jackstays and other clip on points.

Liferaft; how and when to launch and
location of the grab bag.

Accident and injury

Identify danger areas; boom, winches,
clutches, open hatches.

Work on the windward deck, when the
boat is heeled.

Location of first aid kit.

Spares

Where to find extra fuel,
spares and toolkits.

THE BASICS

Throttle and gear control

One lever controls both gear and throttle. Pushing the lever forward or backwards by one click engages gear with engine idling, further movement increases power.

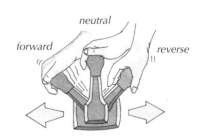

When changing between gears rest the lever in neutral momentarily to reduce the chance of gear crashing.

Rudders

A boat will only react to steering when there is water flowing over the rudder. Flow over the rudder is gained from: the propeller (propwash); the boat moving through the water; or when a stream of water is running over the rudder.

Yacht rudders have a large surface area and are able to steer at very slow speeds.

Turning the rudder and engaging gear throws propwash over one side of the rudder, increasing the rudders effectiveness and turning the boat in a smaller circle.

When going astern, propwash does not flow across the rudder. Steering relies on water flow gained by movment astern.

When manoeuvring in tight spaces, turn the rudder first and then apply power. The propwash from the propeller deflects off the angled rudder and turns the boat in a smaller space.

Pivot points

When a boat turns the bow goes one way and the stern the other. Because of the position of the rudder it is actually the stern of the boat being steered even though the bow is turning.

When motoring ahead a yacht pivots around a point approximately a third from the bow, roughly at the mast.

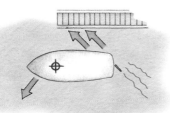

In ahead; beware of colliding with obstructions with your stern.

In astern, the pivot point moves to a point approximately a third from the stern. Monitor the bow, because this is when it will swing the most.

Propellers

Propellers are designed to push the boat forward through the water. Props are handed, either left or right hand, referring to their rotation in forward gear.

right hand propeller

Propwalk

The propeller rotation can also make the stern walk to one side. This action is called propwalk and is more prominent when going astern.

Propwalk can be used to advantage during tight turns and its effect is taken into account during reversing and all manocuvres.

To find propwalk direction, run the engine astern with the boat moored. Prop wash is more visible one side than the other.

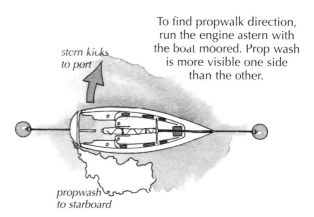

stern kicks to port

propwash to starboard

GOING ASTERN

When going astern the yacht is affected in three ways.

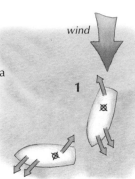

1 The pivot point moves aft to a point a third from the stern. This makes the stern initially seek the wind as bow windage increases.

2 Propwalk may initially kick the stern one way.

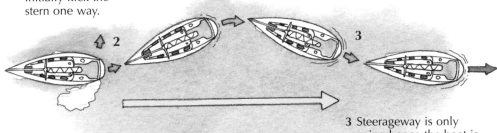

3 Steerageway is only gained once the boat is moving astern.

Start from stopped or slow in the water.

If your boat does not like going astern, start off stern to wind to get it reversing easily.

Use positive power to start with, and then ease off.

Use minimal rudder.

If the yacht sheers excessively, go ahead to stop the boat and start again.

Most modern yachts handle well astern, but some older boats can be difficult.

Use both hands on the wheel or tiller as the steering will be heavy.

Because the bow will travel twice as much as the stern, look forward and backwards to monitor the boat.

Go too fast, or use too much rudder and the tiller or wheel will react violently. This could break the steering mechanism.

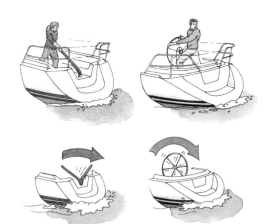

EFFECT OF WIND AND STREAM

Wind and stream have an effect on how the boat reacts when manoeuvring.

Be aware of wind direction. Flags, wind indicators on the mast and wind ruffling the surface of the water are all useful telltales.

A boat that has stopped or is slow moving will drift downwind. Good wind awareness is essential to avoid drifting onto obstructions.

The bow will always drift downwind first as the bow has less grip in the water and more windage than the stern.

wind

wind

The easiest way to hold position in wind is to reverse gently and sit stern to wind. Reversing moves the pivot point aft enabling the bow to easily blow downwind.

Streams

A stream is caused by tide, natural river flow or local movement of water, as around locks. Streams are similar to a conveyor belt, they move you in one direction.

Travel with the stream and travel will be faster past the shore.

Travel against the stream and travel will be slower past the shore.

Travel across the stream and you will be pushed sideways.

When coming alongside, berth into the stream. The boat will be slower over ground with increased water-flow over the rudder.

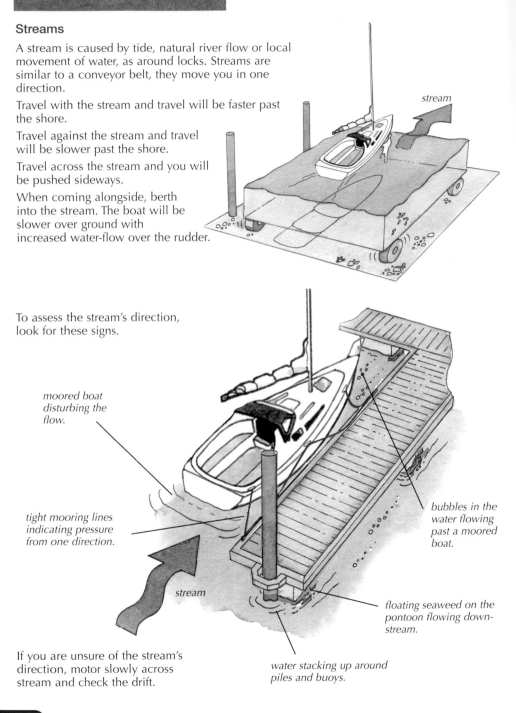

stream

To assess the stream's direction, look for these signs.

moored boat disturbing the flow.

tight mooring lines indicating pressure from one direction.

bubbles in the water flowing past a moored boat.

stream

floating seaweed on the pontoon flowing down-stream.

If you are unsure of the stream's direction, motor slowly across stream and check the drift.

water stacking up around piles and buoys.

JUDGING DRIFT AND SPEED

As a boat slows, drift from a cross stream or crosswind will increase. Use transits to judge this during boat handling.

Drift

When approaching a buoy or a pontoon in a crosswind, select an object beyond it to help judge the drift on the approach.

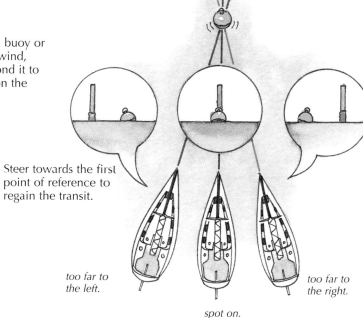

Steer towards the first point of reference to regain the transit.

too far to the left.

spot on.

too far to the right.

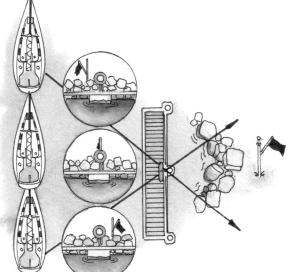

Speed

Find two objects abeam to check your speed over ground.

If there is a lot of stream running an electronic log can register 2-3 knots even when the boat is stationary, only a transit will confirm this.

TIGHT TURNING

For a tight turn; start from stopped in the water, or from very slow speed. Speed carried into a turn increases the turning circle and makes the yacht slide sideways, increasing the radius.

Turning in wind

Turn the bow through the wind. Once the bow is through the wind it helps turn the yacht. This keeps the yacht away from downwind dangers. Try to keep the bow turning throughout the turn.

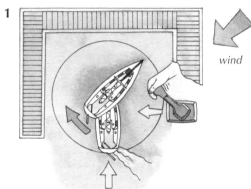

wind

1 Position the boat central to the gap.

Put the rudder hard over and give a short burst of power.

Engage neutral.

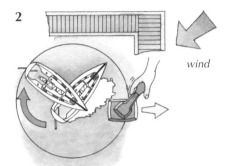

wind

2 Go astern to stop the yacht moving forwards.

Engage neutral.

The rudder can *usually* be left in the same position as steerageway astern is not gained.

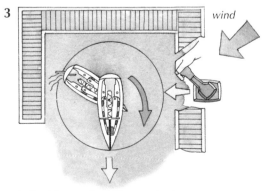

wind

3 A final burst ahead keeps the boat turning. When pointing in the right direction, straighten the helm.

Use of propwalk

The effect of propwalk will either help or hinder a turn in wind. If there is no wind or tide, turn using propwalk to your advantage.

Turning in stream

When turning with a stream running through in a marina aisle turn the bow through the stream.

COMING ALONGSIDE

Good communication between skipper and crew is essential. Make a plan, advise your crew of it and what they will be required to do.

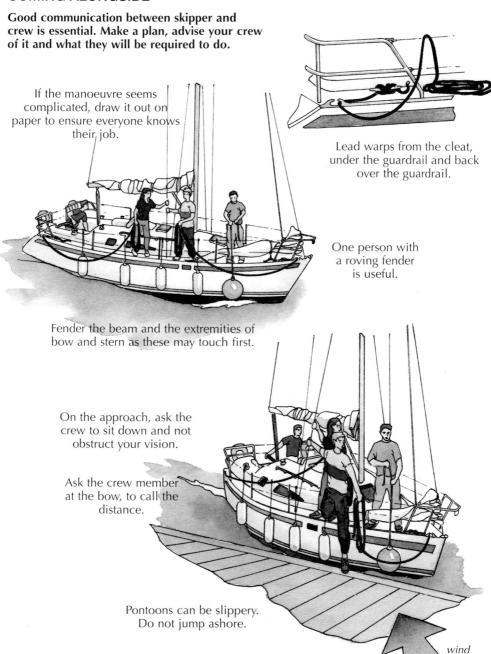

If the manoeuvre seems complicated, draw it out on paper to ensure everyone knows their job.

Lead warps from the cleat, under the guardrail and back over the guardrail.

One person with a roving fender is useful.

Fender the beam and the extremities of bow and stern as these may touch first.

On the approach, ask the crew to sit down and not obstruct your vision.

Ask the crew member at the bow, to call the distance.

Pontoons can be slippery. Do not jump ashore.

wind

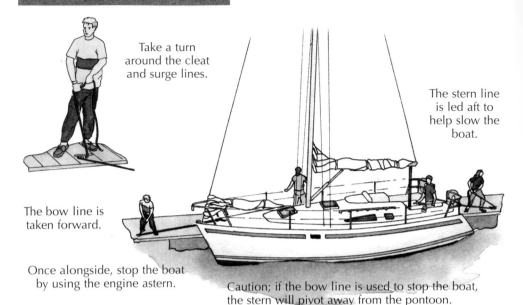

Take a turn around the cleat and surge lines.

The stern line is led aft to help slow the boat.

The bow line is taken forward.

Once alongside, stop the boat by using the engine astern.

Caution; if the bow line is used to stop the boat, the stern will pivot away from the pontoon.

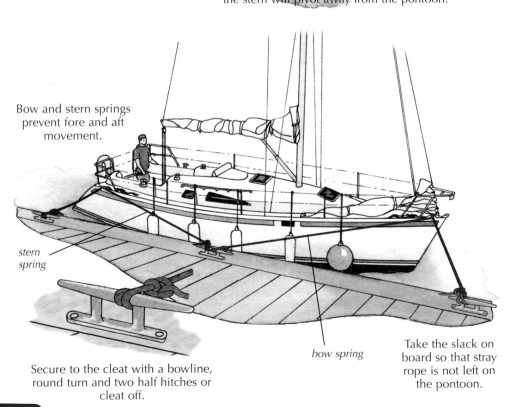

Bow and stern springs prevent fore and aft movement.

stern spring

bow spring

Secure to the cleat with a bowline, round turn and two half hitches or cleat off.

Take the slack on board so that stray rope is not left on the pontoon.

ASSESSING THE SITUATION

The direction and strength of wind and stream will change in different areas of a harbour or marina. Assess the conditions in the marina berth before committing to an approach. Carry out a trial run and have an escape route just in case. Brief the crew and have fenders and warps in place before starting an approach.

Look for signs of wind and stream before entry.

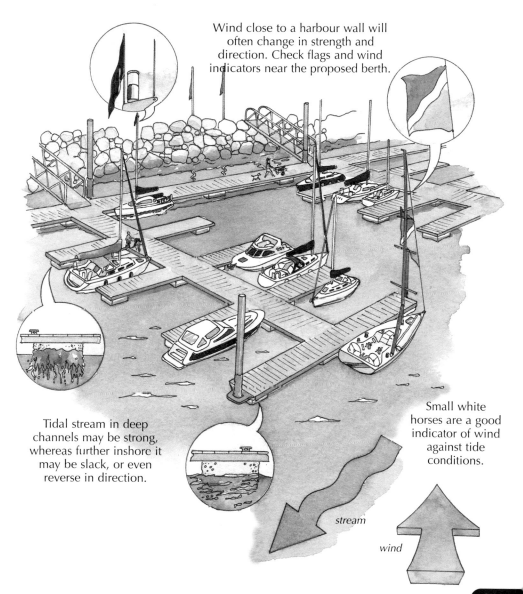

Wind close to a harbour wall will often change in strength and direction. Check flags and wind indicators near the proposed berth.

Tidal stream in deep channels may be strong, whereas further inshore it may be slack, or even reverse in direction.

Small white horses are a good indicator of wind against tide conditions.

stream

wind

BASIC APPROACHES

Approach at the slowest speed that will allow steerageway and control. Usually only the boat's momentum and idle ahead is required.

No wind or tide

Aim for a point at the front of the berth.

Approach at a shallow angle.

Use idle ahead or neutral.

When close to the pontoon, steer the stern in parallel.

Go astern to stop.

Onshore wind

Aim forward of the berth to prevent being blown downwind too early.

To counteract the bow blowing downwind, steer away from the pontoon and go ahead to keep the boat parallel.

Let the wind blow the boat alongside.

Go astern to stop once the fenders touch.

wind

Offshore wind

An offshore wind requires a positive approach so fender the bow.

Aim at the centre or first third of the berth.

When about one metre away, steer parallel to the berth.

The boat should slide alongside.

Get warps ashore promptly and go astern to stop.

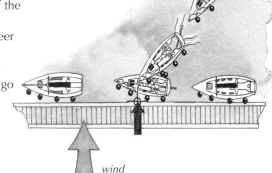

wind

BERTHING IN A STREAM

The presence of stream will be the key factor in planning an approach.

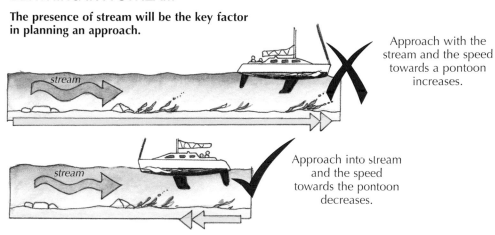

Approach with the stream and the speed towards a pontoon increases.

Approach into stream and the speed towards the pontoon decreases.

An approach into stream allows the slowest approach and greatest control due to increasing water flow over the rudder without increasing speed. Judge speed by looking at points abeam.

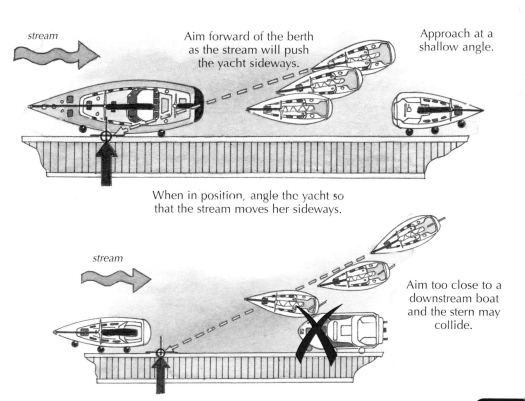

Aim forward of the berth as the stream will push the yacht sideways.

Approach at a shallow angle.

When in position, angle the yacht so that the stream moves her sideways.

Aim too close to a downstream boat and the stern may collide.

Ferry gliding

Ferry gliding is a useful way to get into a tight berth when stream is present. The term describes stemming the stream and making the yacht crab sideways into a berth.

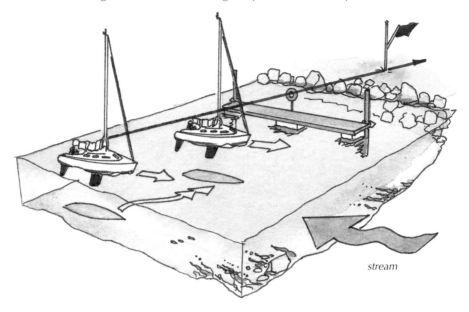

stream

Stemming the stream is achieved by motoring into the stream so that the boat is not moving forwards or backwards - a transit abeam is used to check. To move sideways, keep the transit whilst steering slightly towards the pontoon. Water flowing over the rudder allows steerage and tide pushing on the bow moves the boat sideways.

Berthing with stream

Downstream berthing is difficult. As the boat slows it loses steerageway but it is still being swept towards the pontoon - out of control. If a downstream berth is approached, use the shallowest approach angle possible and get the stern line or an amidships line made fast quickly.

BEWARE
If the approach angle is not shallow enough this can happen.

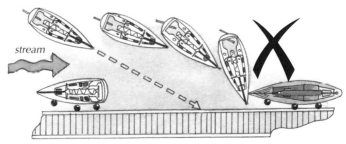

stream

Mooring to a wall

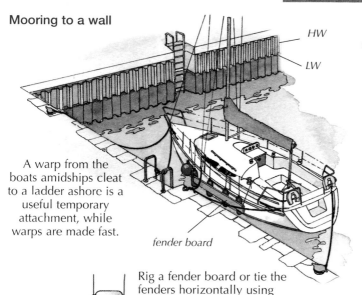

HW

LW

Check there is
sufficient depth
at LW.

Warps should be
adjustable from
the boat.

A warp from the
boats amidships cleat
to a ladder ashore is a
useful temporary
attachment, while
warps are made fast.

fender board

If rise and fall of tidal
height is expected; warp
length should be three
times the range of tide.

Rig a fender board or tie the
fenders horizontally using
an extra piece of line.

Rafting up

Ask the other boats
their departure time.

Rig fenders higher
than for a pontoon.

Check that masts
and spreaders will
not touch.

Once alongside, walk
around the bow of the
other moored boat.

Secure with bow and stern
breast lines then fore and
aft springs.

Lead lines ashore so that
the load of your boat is
not taken by the other.

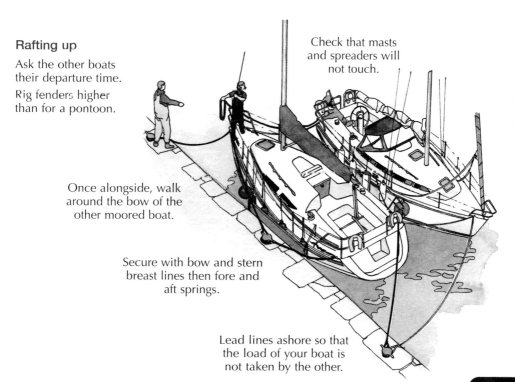

Plan the manoeuvre considering the affects of stream and wind. Brief the crew ensuring everyone knows their role.

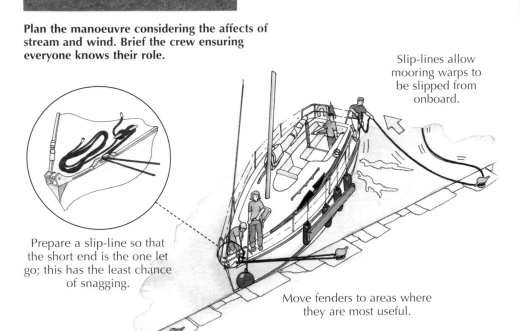

Slip-lines allow mooring warps to be slipped from onboard.

Prepare a slip-line so that the short end is the one let go; this has the least chance of snagging.

Move fenders to areas where they are most useful.

Leaving a raft

It is normal to slip out of a raft down stream. This enables the stream to help close the raft up again.

When the yacht has left, the motor cruiser pulls themselves back alongside and makes fast.

Motor cruiser crew ready to pull in the bow shore line.

New stern line led ashore – round the stern of the departing boat, ready to be hauled-in.

stream

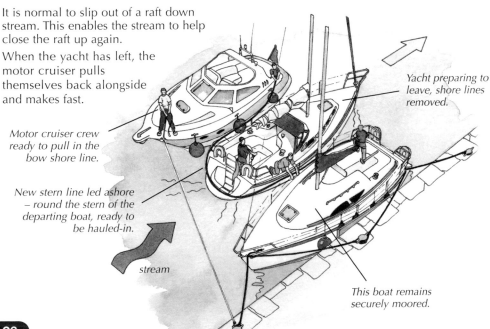

Yacht preparing to leave, shore lines removed.

This boat remains securely moored.

Leaving a finger berth

It is sometimes necessary to get the stern into clear water before reversing away. This will stop the fenders popping out or counteract an onshore wind.

A bow spring will take the stern away from the pontoon before reversing out.

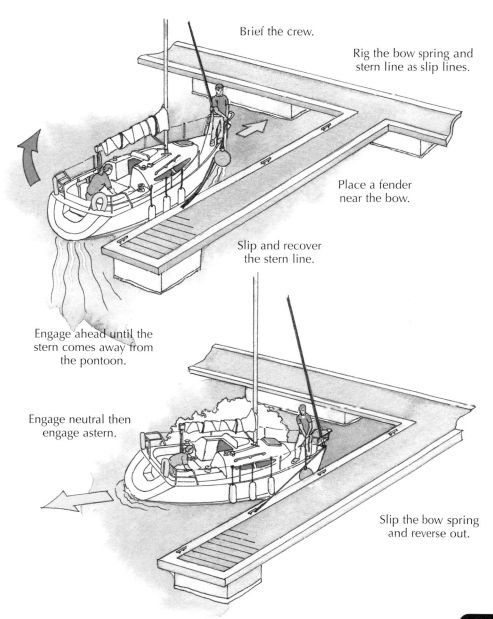

Brief the crew.

Rig the bow spring and stern line as slip lines.

Place a fender near the bow.

Slip and recover the stern line.

Engage ahead until the stern comes away from the pontoon.

Engage neutral then engage astern.

Slip the bow spring and reverse out.

Onshore wind with stream

An onshore wind usually requires the use of a spring to prise the boat off the pontoon. Whether a bow or stern spring is used is dictated by the direction of the stream.

Bow spring

If the stream is from astern use a bow spring.

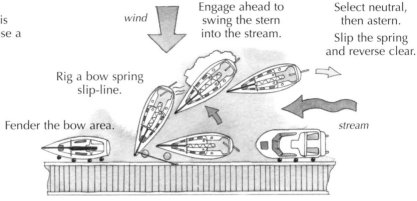

wind

Engage ahead to swing the stern into the stream.

Select neutral, then astern.

Slip the spring and reverse clear.

Rig a bow spring slip-line.

Fender the bow area.

stream

Stern spring

If the stream is from ahead use a stern spring.

Fender the quarter.

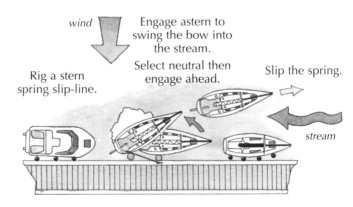

wind

Engage astern to swing the bow into the stream.

Select neutral then engage ahead.

Slip the spring.

Rig a stern spring slip-line.

stream

Offshore wind

The boat will blow clear of the berth and should not require springs.

Slip the bow line.

Allow the bow to blow to the required angle.

Slip the stern line and motor away.

Alternatively, slip the stern line first to allow the stern to blow clear, followed by the bow and motor away.

Rig bow and stern slip-lines.

wind

SCOPE AND SWINGING ROOM

Scope

Remember the basic principles. An anchor works best when the pull from the boat is closest to horizontal.

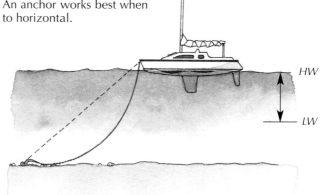

Check the depth and tidal range.

Use a scope (length) of anchor cable at least four times the depth for chain and six times for rope/chain combinations.

If in doubt, let out more.

Swinging circle

More scope and low water will increase the swinging circle.

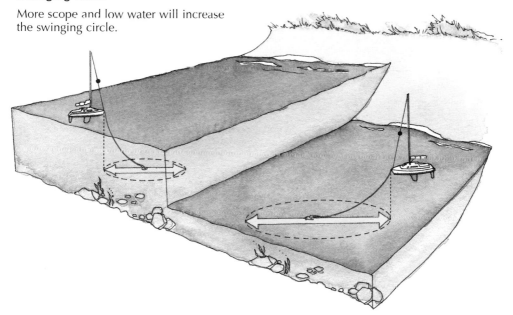

Ensure the maximum swinging circle clears obstructions.

Dropping the anchor

Brief the crew on how to anchor. You may need to demonstrate the use of the windlass.

3 Drift back, or go astern slowly, paying out the scope.

2 Drop the anchor and a third of the scope.

1 Approach into the wind or stream.

4 Let the boat come to rest as the anchor bites.

5 Set the anchor with a short burst of astern power.

Do not drop all the chain at once - it will foul the anchor.

Are we holding?

Establish a transit to check that the boat is not dragging.

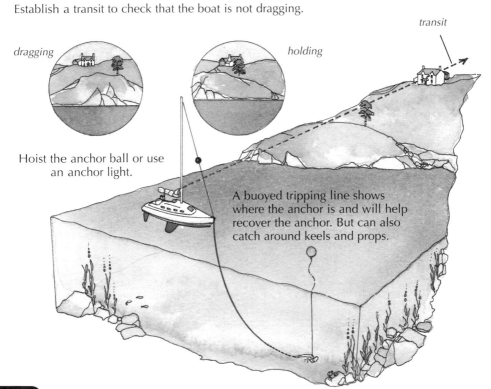

transit

dragging

holding

Hoist the anchor ball or use an anchor light.

A buoyed tripping line shows where the anchor is and will help recover the anchor. But can also catch around keels and props.

Raising the anchor

It is useful to know where the anchor lies when motoring up to it. Ask the crew to point to its location. If the anchorage is muddy, a bucket and brush may be required.

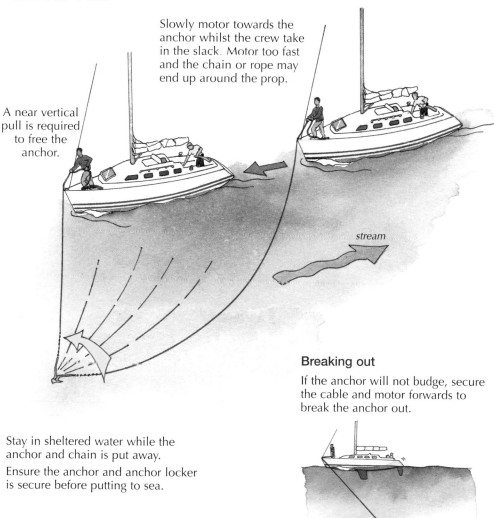

Normally the boat will be lying to either wind or tide.

Slowly motor towards the anchor whilst the crew take in the slack. Motor too fast and the chain or rope may end up around the prop.

A near vertical pull is required to free the anchor.

stream

Breaking out

If the anchor will not budge, secure the cable and motor forwards to break the anchor out.

Stay in sheltered water while the anchor and chain is put away.

Ensure the anchor and anchor locker is secure before putting to sea.

Many areas around the world berth bow or stern to a quay. An anchor or a line to a buoy is used to hold the yacht away from the quay.

wind

Bow-to

Prepare two bow lines and fenders.

Prepare the kedge anchor at the stern. Ensure it is tied on.

Rig fenders on both sides.

Drop the kedge three to four boat lengths from the quay.

Snub the anchor half a boat length out.

At the quay attach the bow lines - windward first.

Tighten in on the kedge.

Lazylines

Some harbours have lazylines secured to an underwater mooring instead of using an anchor.

The lazyline is picked up from the quayside on arrival and led aft. Twin bow lines secure the bow.

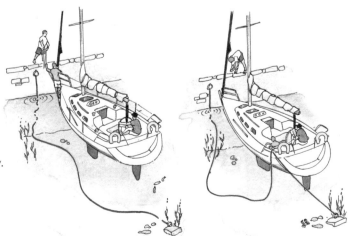

Stern-to offers easier access to the shore, but less privacy. Ensure there are no rocks close to the quay that could damage the rudder.

Stern-to

Rig two stern lines.

Fender both sides and the transom.

Prepare the anchor.

Reverse in and drop the anchor three to four boat lengths from the quay.

Snub the anchor half a boat length from the quay.

Attach the stern lines.

Offshore wind

The stern seeks the wind on the approach – so drop the anchor and slowly reverse to the quay.

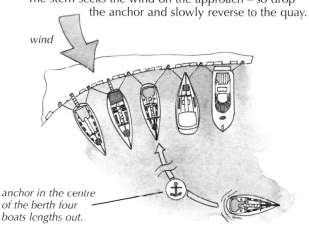

wind

anchor in the centre of the berth four boats lengths out.

Onshore wind

Once the anchor is dropped it will hold the bow head to wind. Either ease back on the chain or reverse in.

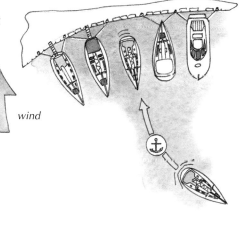

wind

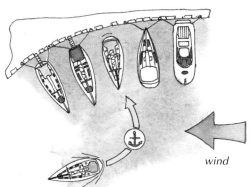

wind

Crosswind

Keep momentum so the crosswind does not drift the boat to leeward.

Initially you will lie alongside the downwind boat.

FIRST PRINCIPLES

The International Rules for the Prevention of Collision at Sea (IRPCS) are legally binding on all vessels and apply to all water users.

Additionally, local harbour by-laws cover speed limits, small craft channels and rules to regulate local marine environments.

The IRPCS rules require all vessels to maintain a lookout at all times.

Remember to look astern.

A sailboat has many blind spots so more vigilance is required.

All vessels have an absolute obligation to avoid a collision. This applies even if you are the stand on vessel, you must avoid a collision if the other vessel is not giving way.

WILL WE COLLIDE

If another vessel is on a constant bearing then a risk of collision exists.

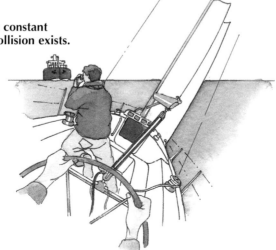

A handbearing compass can be used to check the bearing.

Or line up a stanchion with the other vessel to check if the relative bearing is constant.

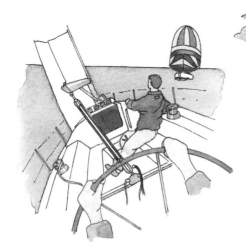

The starboard tack boat is the stand-on vessel but has it been seen by the boat with the spinnaker? Leave action too late and a collision may be unavoidable.

Make your intentions early and clear. A course alteration is always easier to spot than a speed alteration.

VESSELS IN SIGHT OF ONE ANOTHER

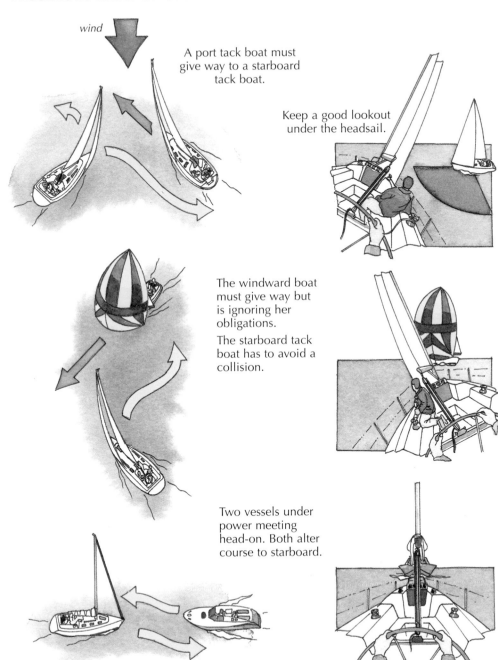

wind

A port tack boat must give way to a starboard tack boat.

Keep a good lookout under the headsail.

The windward boat must give way but is ignoring her obligations.

The starboard tack boat has to avoid a collision.

Two vessels under power meeting head-on. Both alter course to starboard.

Two power driven vessels.
The boat with the motoring cone
has the other on her starboard bow
and must give way.

wind

Power gives way to sail.
(see page 40)

An overtaking boat must keep clear.

She can pass either side
of the slower boat.

NARROW CHANNELS

Here is a typical narrow channel situation. The cargo vessel is in a narrow channel and constrained by her draught. It will expect all other smaller vessels to keep outside the marked channel.

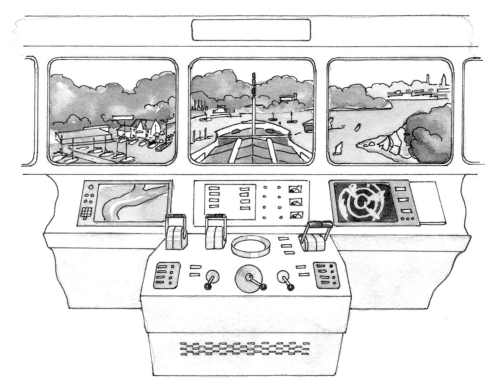

The vessel has a large turning circle and is slow to accelerate, decelerate and stop. Actions have to be planned well ahead and may be irreversible once taken.

Visibility from the bridge is very limited.

Prudent yacht skippers will keep well clear.

Imagine it is your boat that has a draught of ten metres. Now look at the chart again. A wide expanse of water suddenly looks like a very narrow channel.

HIERARCHY

There is a sensible pecking order built into the IRPCS. A more manoeuvrable vessel must not impede the passage of the less manoeuvrable one.

A small power vessel (including a sailing yacht under engine) is at the bottom of the pile.

Operating
engines astern.

SOUND SIGNALS

**Sound signals are used to indicate a
vessel's intentions or concern about
other vessels intentions.**

Turning to
port.

Unsure of your
intentions.

Turning to
starboard.

Restricted visibility

Keep clear of shipping lanes and channels
when visibility is restricted.

Use the correct sound signal.

Large vessels may not hear your signals, seek
shallow water.

Use radar if possible.

Vessels over 12m should carry a bell for use
at anchor.

Good sail trim allows the boat to sail faster and more comfortably. This will make passages quicker and less tiring on the crew.

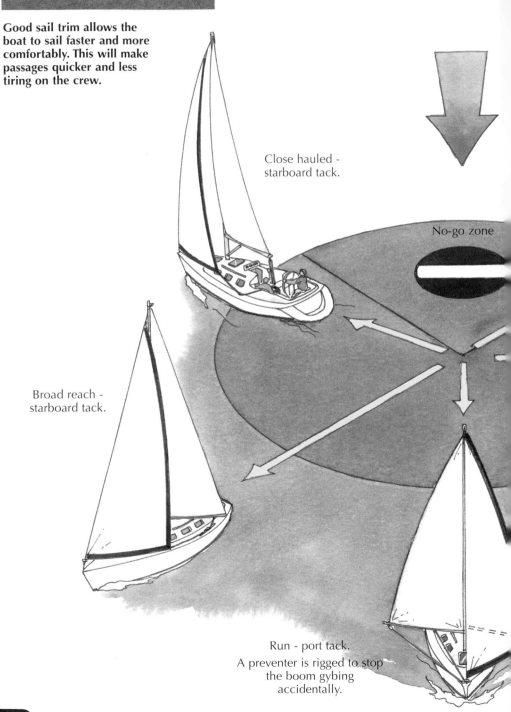

Close hauled - starboard tack.

No-go zone

Broad reach - starboard tack.

Run - port tack.
A preventer is rigged to stop the boom gybing accidentally.

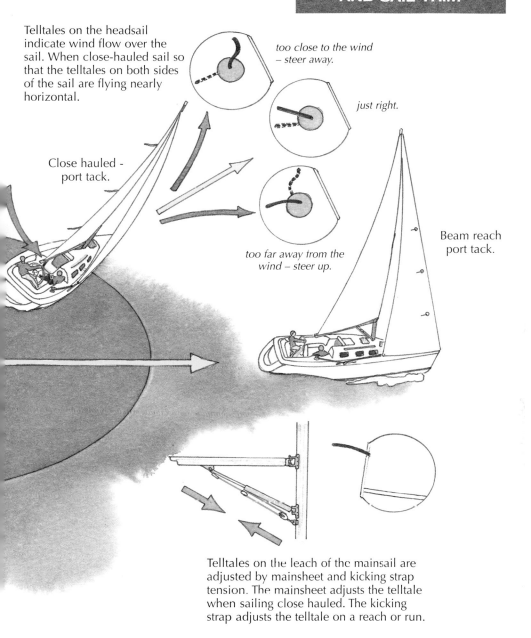

Telltales on the headsail indicate wind flow over the sail. When close-hauled sail so that the telltales on both sides of the sail are flying nearly horizontal.

too close to the wind – steer away.

just right.

Close hauled - port tack.

too far away from the wind – steer up.

Beam reach port tack.

Telltales on the leach of the mainsail are adjusted by mainsheet and kicking strap tension. The mainsheet adjusts the telltale when sailing close hauled. The kicking strap adjusts the telltale on a reach or run.

Make sail changes easier for the crew. Heaving-to is a good way to drop a headsail or put in a reef as it steadies the yacht. If the yacht needs less sail, the crew need a harness.

Roller-furling headsail

Unfurling

Ease the furling line under tension, whilst pulling in on the headsail sheet.

Furling

Ease the sheet whilst hauling in on the furling line. Keep the sheet under a little tension to ensure a smooth furl.

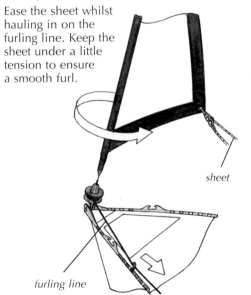

sheet

furling line

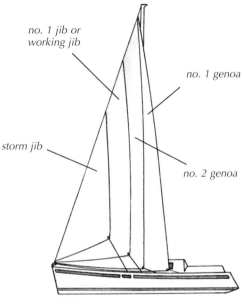

no. 1 jib or working jib

no. 1 genoa

storm jib

no. 2 genoa

When you change the size of the headsail you will also need to change the position of the car (sheeting angle).

Hanked-on jib

You can prepare the new headsail for hoisting before you drop the old one.

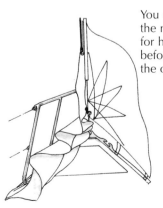

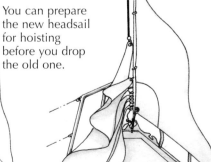

Dropping the headsail

1 Ease the halyard.

2 Pull down on the luff of the sail. Keep some tension on the jib sheet so neither the sail or the sheet go over the side.

Large headsails may need two people on the foredeck to control the sail.

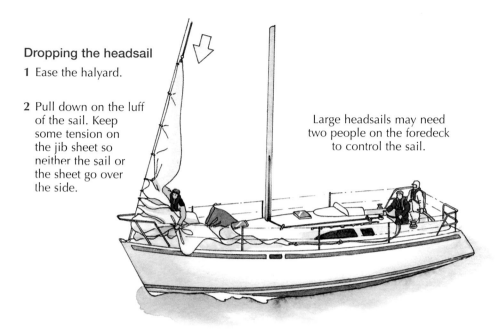

3 Remove the halyard from the sail and clip it onto the pulpit. Re-tension the halyard.

4 Pull the sail back and roll it so that it can be tied to the guard rail to use again.

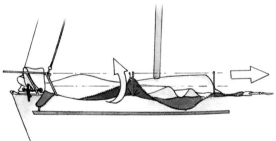

5 Or if not required again, fold it from the clew forward. Remove the hanks and stuff it into its sail bag.

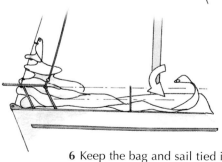

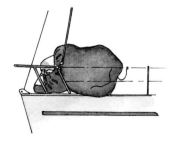

6 Keep the bag and sail tied in place.

7 Coil up and tidy all sheets and the halyard.

To make reefing easier, reduce heeling by easing the sails or heaving-to. If the crew need to go on deck, ensure they are harnessed on and use the windward side of the deck. Close the companionway hatch so the crew do not fall.

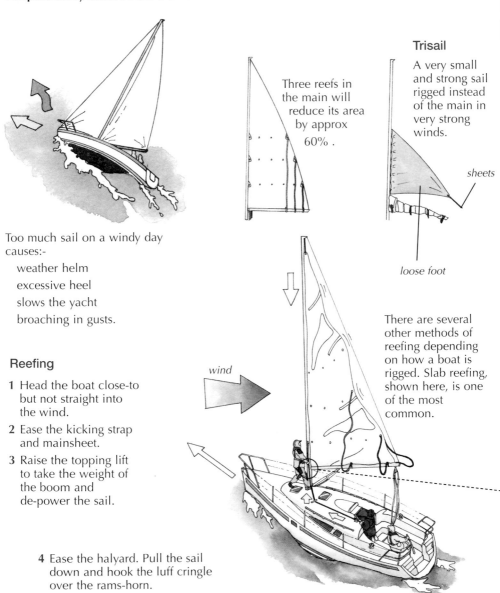

Three reefs in the main will reduce its area by approx 60% .

Trisail

A very small and strong sail rigged instead of the main in very strong winds.

sheets

loose foot

Too much sail on a windy day causes:-

> weather helm
> excessive heel
> slows the yacht
> broaching in gusts.

Reefing

wind

1 Head the boat close-to but not straight into the wind.

2 Ease the kicking strap and mainsheet.

3 Raise the topping lift to take the weight of the boom and de-power the sail.

There are several other methods of reefing depending on how a boat is rigged. Slab reefing, shown here, is one of the most common.

4 Ease the halyard. Pull the sail down and hook the luff cringle over the rams-horn.

5 Winch the halyard tight.

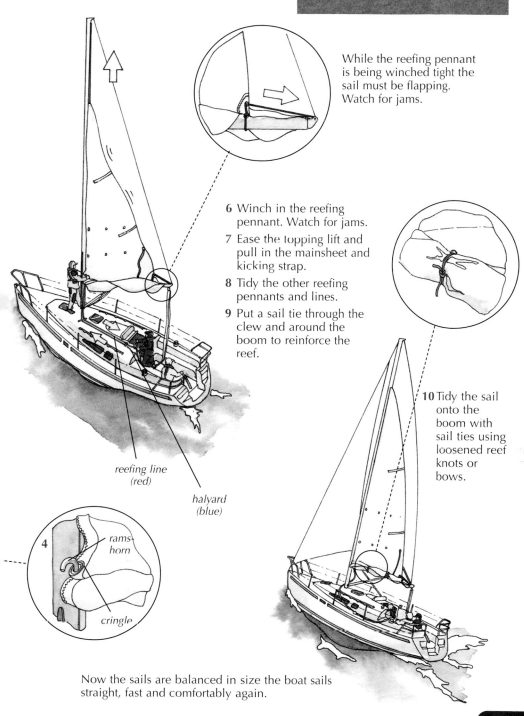

While the reefing pennant is being winched tight the sail must be flapping. Watch for jams.

6 Winch in the reefing pennant. Watch for jams.

7 Ease the topping lift and pull in the mainsheet and kicking strap.

8 Tidy the other reefing pennants and lines.

9 Put a sail tie through the clew and around the boom to reinforce the reef.

10 Tidy the sail onto the boom with sail ties using loosened reef knots or bows.

reefing line (red)

halyard (blue)

4 *rams-horn*

cringle

Now the sails are balanced in size the boat sails straight, fast and comfortably again.

MOORING BUOYS

Wind and stream should be taken into account when sailing up to a mooring buoy. The direction of wind and stream differ from one buoy to the next. If stream is present always moor into stream.

Decision making

Take a trial run past the buoy to; check the depth and the direction of wind and stream.

Decide which sail to use by; sailing past the buoy into stream, letting out both sails, whichever sail does not spill wind, take down and approach with the sail that will spill wind.

mainsail will not spill – take it down, approach under headsail.

if main and headsail flap, use both sails or just the mainsail.

wind

wind

Wind against stream

Approach downwind into the stream using the headsail. Control speed by furling most of the sail away or dropping it.

stream

wind

Wind only

Sail up to the buoy on a close reach under mainsail. Ease the sail to slow down. In light wind, both sails may be required.

Wind with stream

Approach on a close reach under mainsail using the tide as a brake and easing the sail to slow down.

back eddies

wind

stream

tide

stream

CLOSE REACH – STRATEGY

Approach on a close reach (the blue sector in the diagram). This angle allows the mainsail to be eased (spilled) to slow the boat but will also allow it to be powered-up again (filled) if required.

On a beam or broad reach, the mainsail cannot be eased enough to spill the wind.

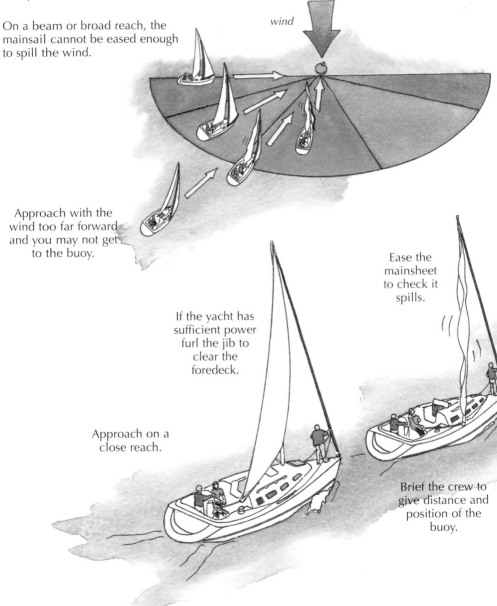

wind

Approach with the wind too far forward and you may not get to the buoy.

Ease the mainsheet to check it spills.

If the yacht has sufficient power furl the jib to clear the foredeck.

Approach on a close reach.

Brief the crew to give distance and position of the buoy.

Filling and spilling

wind

To spill the sail, ease the mainsheet fully and drop the traveller to leeward.

To fill the sail, grab the falls of the mainsheet and lean back.

Pick up the buoy on the windward bow.

Fill and spill the sail up to the buoy.

wind

Aim slightly upwind on the approach to compensate for leeway get the buoy in transit with another fixed object.

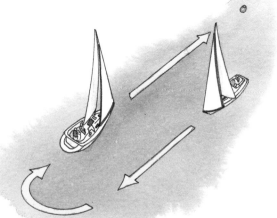

To judge the approach angle when there is little or no stream, sail past the mooring with the wind just aft of the beam. Tack onto your final approach and the wind will be just forward of the beam (a close reach).

WIND AND STREAM

When the wind is on or abaft the beam use the headsail to approach the buoy. It is sometimes possible to use no sail, just the windage of the boat.

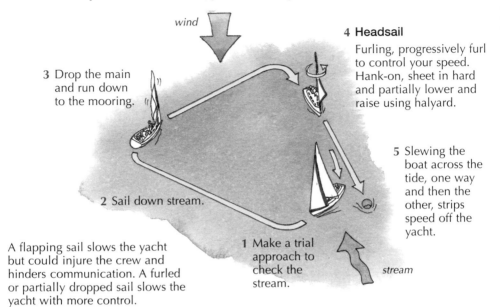

wind

4 Headsail

Furling, progressively furl to control your speed. Hank-on, sheet in hard and partially lower and raise using halyard.

3 Drop the main and run down to the mooring.

5 Slewing the boat across the tide, one way and then the other, strips speed off the yacht.

2 Sail down stream.

1 Make a trial approach to check the stream.

stream

A flapping sail slows the yacht but could injure the crew and hinders communication. A furled or partially dropped sail slows the yacht with more control.

Beam wind approach

Start slightly further upwind to compensate for leeway. Slow by furling or partially dropping the headsail.

wind

stream

Windward pick-up

It is much easier and safer to pick up the buoy from the windward side so that it does not go under the boat.

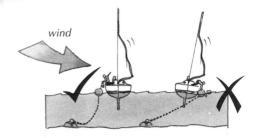

wind

Anchoring under sail is easier than sailing up to a mooring because the anchor is dropped when the boat comes to rest. Give a clear brief and make a trial run to check the depth.

Wind with stream

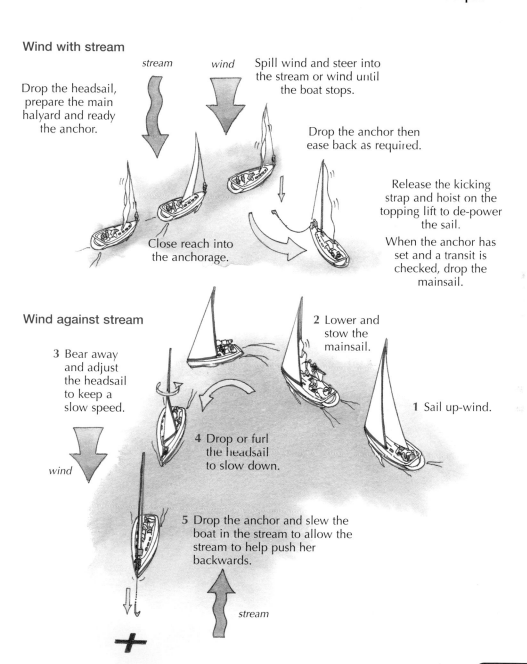

stream *wind*

Drop the headsail, prepare the main halyard and ready the anchor.

Spill wind and steer into the stream or wind until the boat stops.

Drop the anchor then ease back as required.

Close reach into the anchorage.

Release the kicking strap and hoist on the topping lift to de-power the sail.

When the anchor has set and a transit is checked, drop the mainsail.

Wind against stream

3 Bear away and adjust the headsail to keep a slow speed.

2 Lower and stow the mainsail.

1 Sail up-wind.

4 Drop or furl the headsail to slow down.

wind

5 Drop the anchor and slew the boat in the stream to allow the stream to help push her backwards.

stream

The order of initial actions will depend on whether the MOB can be seen and whether the boat can turn straight away.

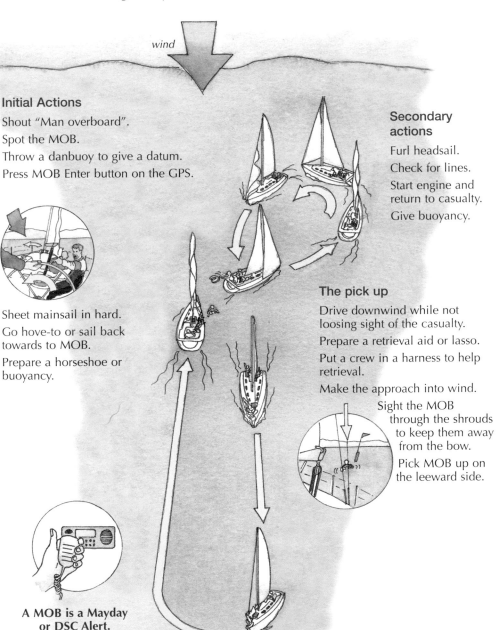

wind

Initial Actions

Shout "Man overboard".

Spot the MOB.

Throw a danbuoy to give a datum.

Press MOB Enter button on the GPS.

Sheet mainsail in hard.

Go hove-to or sail back towards to MOB.

Prepare a horseshoe or buoyancy.

Secondary actions

Furl headsail.

Check for lines.

Start engine and return to casualty.

Give buoyancy.

The pick up

Drive downwind while not loosing sight of the casualty.

Prepare a retrieval aid or lasso.

Put a crew in a harness to help retrieval.

Make the approach into wind.

Sight the MOB through the shrouds to keep them away from the bow.

Pick MOB up on the leeward side.

A MOB is a Mayday or DSC Alert.

GETTING THE MOB ON BOARD

Getting a wet and fully clothed person aboard is not easy. Work out a method and discuss it with your crew so that they will know what to do.

A lasso maybe the easiest way to attach a line to a person in the water.

Muscles loose their strength very quickly in cold water - do not rely on any help from the MOB.

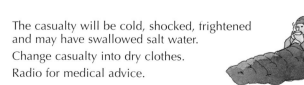

A halyard and two-speed winch or mainsheet will provide a solution.

In calm conditions a boarding ladder may be easiest.

The casualty will be cold, shocked, frightened and may have swallowed salt water.

Change casualty into dry clothes.

Radio for medical advice.

Keep them warm. If possible place them in a sleeping bag.

Head for the nearest port.

Monitor their condition.

A Mayday call is for 'grave and imminent danger' to person or vessel.

Some yachts have VHF radios where all MAYDAY communication is by voice. Others have DSC/VHF radios (Digital Selective Calling) where the initial alert is made by pushing a red emergency button.

VHF/DSC alert

Press the red emergency button for five seconds to send the alert. The message will contain the vessels MMSI number (similar to a phone number), which may contain position and time. Follow up with a MAYDAY by voice.

Voice message

Select channel 16. Press the transmit button on microphone when speaking and remember to release it when you have finished.

MAYDAY CALL

"MAYDAY, MAYDAY, MAYDAY
This is yacht Puffin, yacht Puffin, yacht Puffin
MAYDAY yacht Puffin"

MAYDAY MESSAGE

"MAYDAY yacht Puffin (MMSI)
In position (give latitude and longitude from GPS or position from a known point)
Nature of distress
Number of persons on board
Require immediate assistance
Other VITAL information (abandoning to liferaft/have no liferaft)
OVER"

Buoyant orange smoke

Daylight use only.
Use within three
miles of a rescuer.
Throw downwind.

Cloud lasts three
or four minutes.

wind

Orange hand-held smoke

Cloud lasts
approximately
one minute.

wind

Orange smoke is easy for a
rescue helicopter to see.

Hold by the
handle only, as
the metal casing
gets very hot.

Red hand-held flare

Use day or night
within three miles
of a rescuer.

wind

Hold the flare downwind
and horizontally to
protect your hands.

Red parachute rocket

Remove
cap

10° downwind

Do not use
if a rescue
helicopter is
nearby.

wind

Let off two
rockets so that
the observer can
take a bearing.

All brands of flare operate differently. Read the
instructions before they are needed in a real
emergency. Check flares are in date.

Only use the liferaft if there is no hope of saving the boat. If possible, stay with the boat.

Liferafts are supplied in a canister or valise. A canister is stowed on deck and a valise is kept in a locker opening onto the deck.

wind

Get the crew ready in lifejackets. Send a Mayday.

Check the painter is tied on.

Pull on the painter to inflate the liferaft.

Launch the liferaft on the leeward side.

Climb into the raft, try to keep dry. Do not jump into the water.

For stability get the heaviest adult into the liferaft first.

Take extras; EPIRB, water, carbohydrate foods, first aid kit, warm clothes, sleeping bags, TPA (thermal protection aid) and a hand-held VHF.

Cut the painter and when clear, stream the drogue to increase stability and reduce drift. Keep dry and take anti-seasickness tablets. Ventilate the raft every 30 minutes.

**The helicopter pilot will make contact by VHF and give a brief.
The brief may include a course and speed for you to follow.
Listen carefully and take notes.**

wind

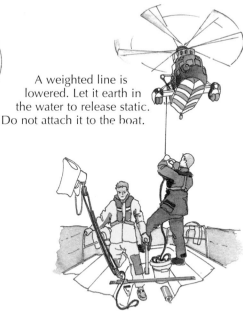

A weighted line is lowered. Let it earth in the water to release static. Do not attach it to the boat.

It is important to steer a constant course without deviating.

Use the line to guide the helicopter winch-man. Gloves are useful.

The winchman will land on deck, unhook, and assess the situation.

The winchman will take the casualty off the boat - the weighted line is used to control his swing.

Tow astern

Tow another vessel from astern if you are at sea in open water.

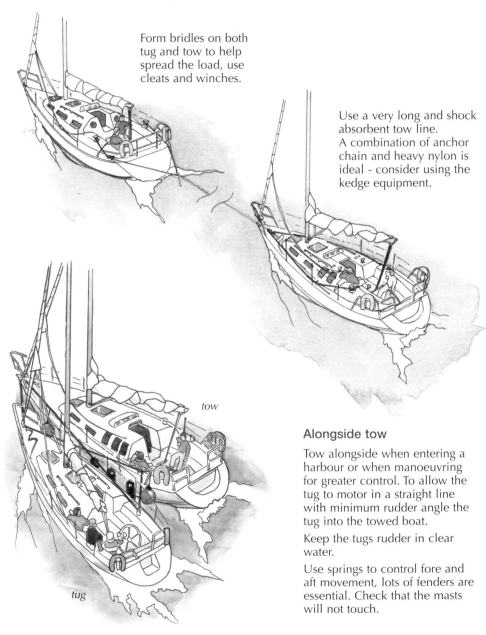

Form bridles on both tug and tow to help spread the load, use cleats and winches.

Use a very long and shock absorbent tow line. A combination of anchor chain and heavy nylon is ideal - consider using the kedge equipment.

tow

tug

Alongside tow

Tow alongside when entering a harbour or when manoeuvring for greater control. To allow the tug to motor in a straight line with minimum rudder angle the tug into the towed boat.

Keep the tugs rudder in clear water.

Use springs to control fore and aft movement, lots of fenders are essential. Check that the masts will not touch.

Causes and action to take

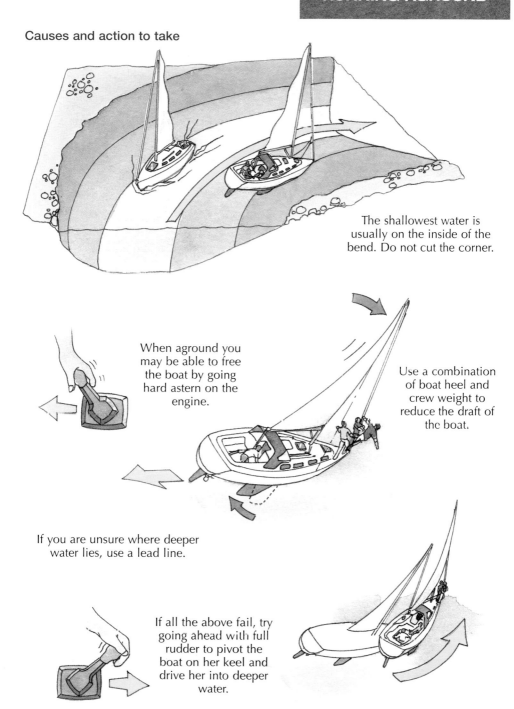

The shallowest water is usually on the inside of the bend. Do not cut the corner.

When aground you may be able to free the boat by going hard astern on the engine.

Use a combination of boat heel and crew weight to reduce the draft of the boat.

If you are unsure where deeper water lies, use a lead line.

If all the above fail, try going ahead with full rudder to pivot the boat on her keel and drive her into deeper water.

When planning a passage consider these points;

How far....
Constraints
Weather
Departure time
Pilotage
Navigation

How far

Passage from Porth Dinllaen to Caernarfon:

Overall journey distance	17 Miles
Boat speed approx	5 Knots
Approximate journey time	3^1/$_2$ Hours

Constraints

Check the chart and pilot books for constraints or tidal gates.

This passage has two tidal constraints.

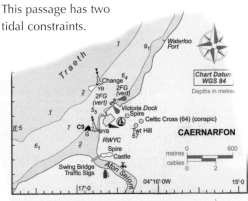

CAERNARFON 53°08'·51N 04°16'·83W ⊛⊛◊◊◊◊✿✿✿
SHELTER Good in Victoria Dock marina, access HW±2 via gates,
trfc lts; pontoons at SW end in 2m. Or in river hbr (S of consp
castle), dries to mud/gravel, access HW±3 via swing brid
opening sound B (−···). ‡ off Foel Ferry, with loca'
or temp ‡ in fair holding off Abermenai Pi
ut strong streams

1 **The entrance to Caernarfon.** The pilot book states Caernarfon is entered via gates and accessed HW ±2hrs.

Find out the time of HW for Caernarfon. (See *Day Skipper Shorebased Notes* for details of Primary and Secondary Ports).

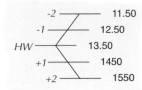

2	Time	m
	07.16	0.6
Sa	12.50	5.0

LW 07.16 +1hr DST (Daylight Saving Time)
HW 12.50 +1hr DST

-2	11.50
-1	12.50
HW	13.50
+1	1450
+2	1550

Caernarfon gates are accessed between 11.50 and 15.50

2 **The Caernarfon Bar.** A note on the chart states that the Bar should only be crossed HW ±3hrs.

DEPTHS

Depths in the entrance to the Menai Strait are continually changing. The buoys are moved accordingly. The entrance should only be used 3 hours either side of High Water. Information concerning the latest positions of the buoys can be obtained from the Harbour Master at Caernarfon.

The Bar is passable between 10.50 and 16.50.

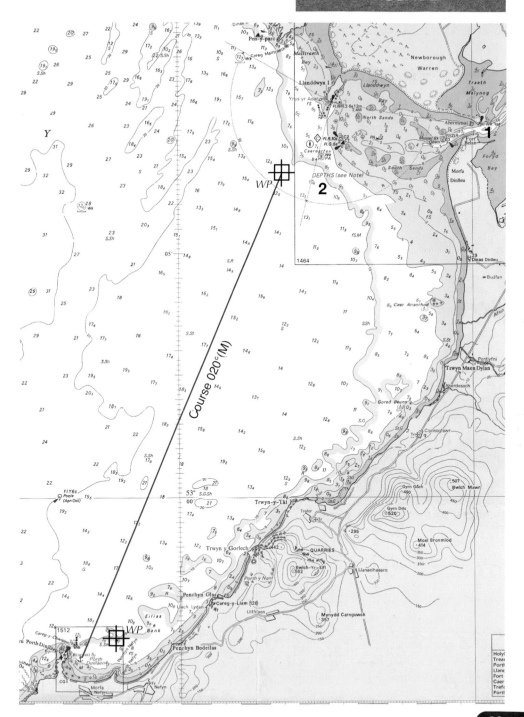

ESTIMATING TIME OF DEPARTURE

When will the tidal stream be favourable?

The distance from Porth Dinlläen to the Bar is 12 miles ($2^{1}/_{2}$ hours).

The distance from the Bar entrance to Caernarfon is 5 miles (1 hour).

Tides based on HW Caernarfon

5 hours before HW Caernarfon

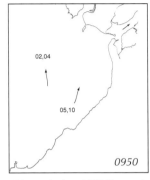

4 hours before HW Caernarfon

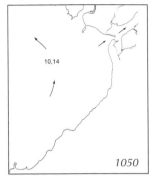

3 hours before HW Caernarfon

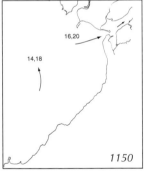

2 hours before HW Caernarfon

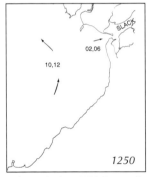

1 hours before HW Caernarfon

HW Caernarfon

Use either a tidal atlas or tidal diamonds. A tidal atlas is easier to interpret.

The new incoming tide starts from Porth Dinlläen from about 0900 onwards.

To find the 'Time To Go' work backwards from the time we need to reach Caernarfon.

The tide starts to turn in the Straits at HW (1350) therefore we need to arrive earlier at 1300 with the last of the incoming tide.

Working backwards from Caernarfon;

1300   Arrive Caernarfon

1200   Entrance at the Bar

0930   Sails up - sailing out of Porth Dinlläen

0915   Anchor up

PILOTAGE

Plan the pilotage before you leave. This is easier done when stationary, than heeled over at 20 degrees and feeling seasick. Simplify the chart to the main points required for entry and exit, i.e. Porth Dinllaen, the Bar and Caernarfon require plans.

When piloting; let someone else helm, so you have time to look at the pilotage plan and to make decisions.

Speed; the boat should travel slower than the speed at which you can make decisions. Think two steps ahead; if you need to, slow down to assess the situation.

Porth Dinllaen Pilotage

Exiting Porth Dinllaen should be straightforward. Rocks to the north are well marked by an Isolated Danger mark.

The danger is the rock awash. To clear the rock awash we could:

• Place a waypoint on the rock and set a proximity/waypoint arrival alarm for 400 yards. If the alarm sounds, stop or alter course.

• Run a clearing line from the flag post on the Coast Guard lookout.

• Crossing the 10m depth contour will notify the clearance of the rock.

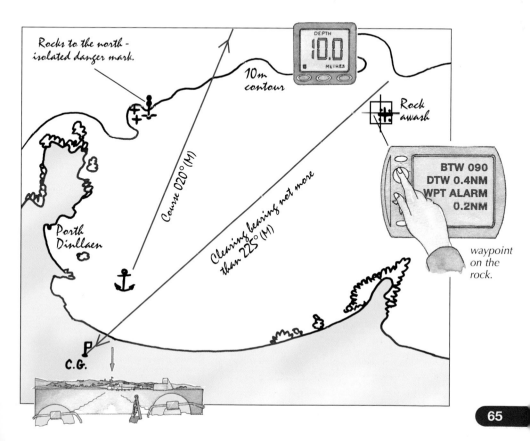

Caernarfon bar pilotage

It is essential the boat stays in the narrow channel through the sandbanks. Even though the buoyed passage looks simple to follow, it is easy to miss a mark and drive onto a bank. Plot a course from buoy to buoy and cross them off as they are passed.

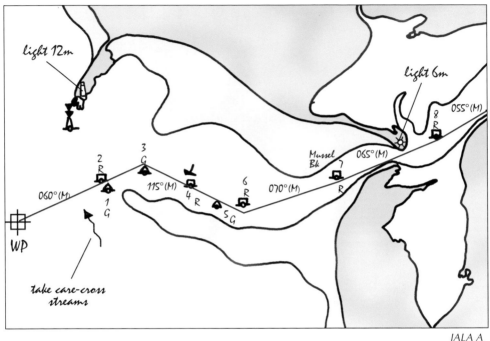

IALA A

Watch for cross streams at a harbour entrance. The compass course could allow the boat to be swept onto a sandbank. Get the next buoy in transit with land behind it to keep a good course over ground. Draw expected cross streams on the plan as a reminder.

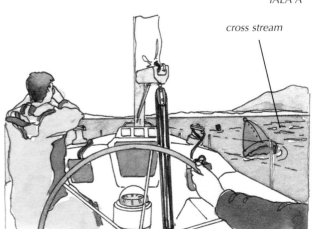

cross stream

NAVIGATION

The forecast of SW 3 with long sunny periods should allow an easy sail and direct course up the Lleyn Peninsula. A course to steer allowing for tide may need working up. (See *Day Skipper Shorebased Notes*).

Plot a waypoint for the Bar on the chart. Enter the waypoint into the GPS and double-check the data.

A useful technique is to draw a waypoint web on the chart so that your position from the waypoint is easily plotted.

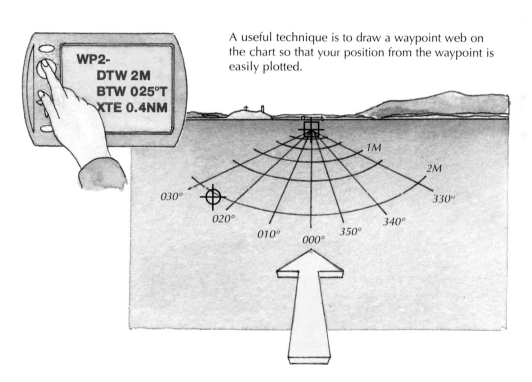

WP2-
DTW 2M
BTW 025°T
XTE 0.4NM

1M
2M
030°
020°
010°
000°
350°
340°
330°

RUNNING THE PASSAGE

Obtain the latest forecast. Be prepared to change your plans and stay in port.

If the forecast is good, leave promptly. Hoist sails in the shelter of the land.

Delegate tasks, do not try and do everything yourself. This will keep everyone interested in the passage and allows them to learn too. Log your position every hour.

Successful arrival at Caernarfon, early due to a fair tide. Watch out for cross tides at the entrance. Consult the Pilot book for details on calling the harbour master.

It is never advisable to set out in fog. However if you are caught out:

Fix your position.

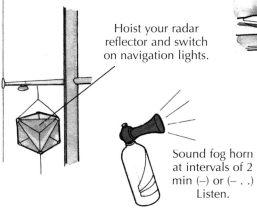

Hoist your radar reflector and switch on navigation lights.

Sound fog horn at intervals of 2 min (–) or (– . .) Listen.

Muster crew on deck in life jackets.

Listen on port frequency to check for commercial traffic.

If there is any likelihood of commercial shipping in your vicinity monitor channel 13 (bridge to bridge channel).

If you have radar keep a constant experienced radar watch.

Navigation strategy

❶ Get out of shipping lanes.

❷ Find and follow contour.

❸ Consider anchoring in shallow water clear of traffic.

Where possible, do not set a course directly for the entrance to a port.

Error may take you to the wrong side putting yourself directly in the path of commercial vessels.

IALA A buoyage

BEAUFORT FORCE

The Beaufort wind scale is the standard way to assess wind strength.

1 **Light airs** 1 - 3 knots.
Ripples.
Sail - drifting conditions.

2 **Light breeze** 4 - 6 knots.
Small wavelets.
Sail - full mainsail and large genoa.

3 **Gentle breeze** 7 - 10 knots.
Occasional crests.
Sail - full sail.

4 **Moderate** 11 - 16 knots.
Frequent white horses.
Sail - reduce headsail size.

5 **Fresh breeze** 17 - 21 knots.
Moderate waves, many white crests.
Sail - reef mainsail.

6 **Strong breeze** 22 - 27 knots.
Large waves, white foam crests.
Sail - reef main and reduce headsail.

7 **Near gale** 28 - 33 knots.
Sea heaps up, spray, breaking waves, foam blows in streaks.
Sail - deep reefed main, small jib.

8 **Gale** 34 - 40 knots.
Moderately high waves, breaking crests.
Sail - deep reefed main, storm jib.

9 **Severe gale** 41 - 47 knots
High waves, spray affects visibility.
Sail - trysail and storm jib.

10 **Storm** 48 - 55 knots.
Very high waves, long breaking crests.
Survival conditions.

NORTHERN HEMISPHERE

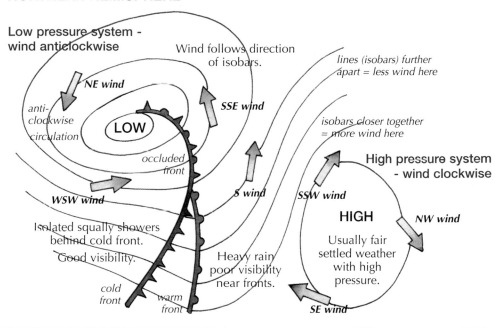

Low pressure system -
wind anticlockwise

Wind follows direction
of isobars.

*lines (isobars) further
apart = less wind here*

NE wind

*anti-
clockwise
circulation*

LOW

SSE wind

*isobars closer together
= more wind here*

*occluded
front*

High pressure system
- wind clockwise

WSW wind

S wind

SSW wind

NW wind

HIGH

Isolated squally showers
behind cold front.
Good visibility.

Usually fair
settled weather
with high
pressure.

Heavy rain
poor visibility
near fronts.

*cold
front*

*warm
front*

SE wind

SOUTHERN HEMISPHERE

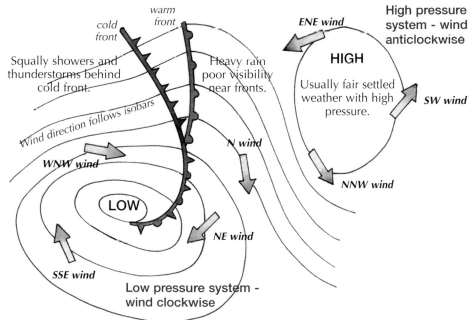

*warm
front*

*cold
front*

ENE wind

High pressure
system - wind
anticlockwise

Squally showers and
thunderstorms behind
cold front.

Heavy rain
poor visibility
near fronts.

HIGH

Usually fair settled
weather with high
pressure.

Wind direction follows isobars

N wind

SW wind

WNW wind

LOW

NNW wind

NE wind

SSE wind

Low pressure system -
wind clockwise

SHIPPING FORECAST AREAS

Get to know your local forecast areas

There are many different ways to obtain a forecast.

Marine safety information broadcasts on VHF by Coastguard.

Metfax

Short message service (SMS).

Recorded forecasts by phone.

Most harbour and marina offices.

Details of forecast times etc. can be found in an almanac or the RYA's *Weather Forecasts book (G5)*

Internet

Teletext

Local radio stations.

TERMS USED IN FORECASTS

Gale warnings	If average wind is expected to be F8 or more, or gusts 43-51kn.
Strong wind warnings	If average wind is expected to be F6 or F7. F6 is often called a 'yachtsman's gale'.
Imminent	Within 6 hrs of time of issue of warning.
Soon	Within 6-12 hrs of time of issue of warning.
Later	More than 12 hrs from time of issue of warning.
Visibility	*Good* - greater than 5 miles *Moderate* - between 2-5 miles. *Poor* - 1,000m to 2 miles. Fog less than 1,000m.
Fair	No significant precipitation.
Backing	Wind changing in an anticlockwise direction eg NW to SW.
Veering	Wind changing in a clockwise direction eg NE to SE.
General synopsis	How and where the weather systems are moving.
Sea states	*Smooth* - wave height 0.2-0.5m *Slight* - wave height 0.5-1.25m. *Moderate* - wave height 1.25-2.5m *Rough* - wave height 2.5-4m. *Very rough* - wave height 4-6m.

Sea breeze

Land breeze

In fair weather and light to moderate offshore wind, a sea breeze is likely to develop. Warm air rises over land, it then cools, descends and blows onshore, generally up to force 4 in strength.

This occurs on a clear night when the air cools over land and flows downhill and out to sea, particularly from river estuaries.

Wind usually no more than force 2-3 except near mountains.

PLANNING THE DAY

Good skippering is all about making a good judgement on the weather and being considerate to your crew.

"Here is the inshore forecast issued at 0700 UT and valid till 0700 tomorrow. Winds South force 3 backing South East for a time then veering SW or W and increasing force 5 to 6, perhaps 7 by dusk. Weather fair, rain later".

Two boats start with the same basic weather information at 0730. Both decide to go for the day but make different decisions on timings.

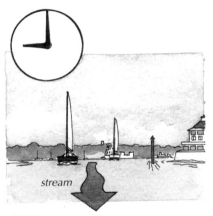

0900

It's a lovely morning and two boats are heading out of harbour taking the last of the ebbing tide.

They enjoy a short beat to a sheltered anchorage.

1200

... and a pleasant lunch. One skipper, remembering the forecast, is keeping a careful eye on the weather.

1500

As the wind backs into the SE he recognises the signs of an approaching weather front and decides now is a good time to return to base...

1700

As the wind increases the skipper of the blue boat faces a problem. Increasing wind makes weighing the anchor and hoisting sail unnecessarily difficult in the now exposed anchorage.

stream

... and takes the last of the tide back into the harbour with a SE wind and has a flat sea state.

stream

The wind veers and increases as forecast. They face a hard beat home in deteriorating weather, against the ebb tide.

NOTES

RYA *Membership*

Promoting and Protecting Boating
www.rya.org.uk

RYA Membership

The RYA is the national organisation which represents the interests of everyone who goes boating for pleasure.

The greater the membership, the louder our voice when it comes to protecting members' interests.

Apply for membership today, and support the RYA, to help the RYA support you.

BENEFITS OF MEMBERSHIP

- Special members' discounts on a range of products and services including boat insurance, books, charts, DVD's and class certificates
- Access to expert advice on all aspects of boating from legal wrangles to training matters
- Free issue of Certificates of Competence, increasingly asked for by everyone from overseas governments to holiday companies, insurance underwriters to boat hirers
- Access to the wide range of RYA publications,including the quarterly magazine
- Third Party insurance for windsurfing members
- Free Internet access with RYA-Online
- Special discounts on AA membership
- Regular offers in RYA Magazine
- ...and much more

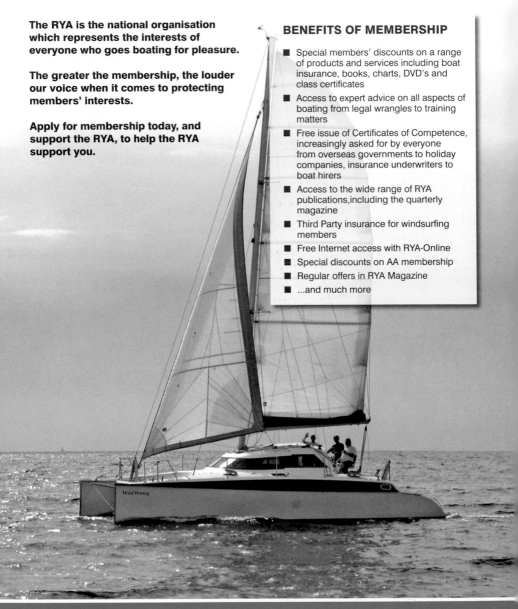

JOIN NOW
Membership form opposite or join online at www.rya.org.uk
Visit our website for information, advice, members' services and web shop.

IT'S ALL ABOUT YOU AND THE BOATING YOU DO

RYA MEMBERSHIP APPLICATION

One of boating's biggest attractions is its freedom from rules and regulations. As an RYA member you'll play an active part in keeping it that way, as well as benefiting from free expert advice and information, plus discounts on a wide range of boating products, charts and publications.

To join the RYA, please complete the application form below and send it to The Membership Department, RYA, RYA House, Ensign Way, Hamble, Southampton, Hampshire SO31 4YA. You can also join online at www.rya.org.uk, or by phoning the membership department on +44 (0) 23 8060 4159. Whichever way you choose to apply, you can save money by paying by Direct Debit. A Direct Debit instruction is on the back of this form.

RYA
Be part of it

	Title	Forename	Surname	Gender	Date of Birth
Applicant ❶					DD / MM / YYYY
Applicant ❷					DD / MM / YYYY
Applicant ❸					DD / MM / YYYY
Applicant ❹					DD / MM / YYYY

Address

Post Code

E-mail Applicant ❶	
E-mail Applicant ❷	
E-mail Applicant ❸	
E-mail Applicant ❹	

Home Tel   Day Time Tel   Mobile Tel

Type of membership required (Tick Box)

Junior (0-11)	Annual rate £5 or **£5 if paying by Direct Debit**
Youth (12-17)	Annual rate £14 or **£11 if paying by Direct Debit**
Under 25	Annual rate £25 or **£22 if paying by Direct Debit**
Personal	Annual rate £45 or **£39 if paying by Direct Debit**
Family*	Annual rate £63 or **£59 if paying by Direct Debit**

Save money by completing the Direct Debit form overleaf

Please number up to three boating interests in order, with number one being your principal interest

Yacht Racing	Yacht Cruising	Dinghy Racing	Dinghy Cruising
Personal Watercraft	Sportboats & RIBs	Windsurfing	Motor Boating
Powerboat Racing	Canal Cruising	River Cruising	

* Family Membership. 2 adults plus any under 18s all living at the same address. Prices valid until 30/9/2011 One discount voucher is accepted for individual memberships, and two discount vouchers are accepted for family membership.

IMPORTANT In order to provide you with membership benefits the details provided by you on this form and in the course of your membership will be maintained on a database. If you do not wish to receive information on member services and benefits please tick here ☐. By applying for membership of the RYA you agree to be bound by the RYA's standard terms and conditions (copies on request or at www.rya.org.uk)

Signature

Date   DD / MM / YYYY

Source Code

Joining Point Code

GET MORE FROM

YOUR
BOATING
SUPPORT THE
RYA

RYA
Be part of it

PAY BY DIRECT DEBIT – AND SAVE MONEY

Instructions to your Bank or Building Society to pay by Direct Debit

Please fill in the form and send to:
Membership Department, Royal Yachting Association, RYA House, Ensign Way, Hamble,
Southampton, Hampshire SO31 4YA.

Name and full postal address of your Bank/Building Society

To the Manager _____ Bank/Building Society

Address _____

_____ Postcode _____

Name(s) of Account Holder(s)

_____

_____

Branch Sort Code

☐☐ – ☐☐ – ☐☐

Bank/Building Society Account Number

☐☐☐☐☐☐☐☐

DIRECT Debit

Originator's Identification Number

9	5	5	2	1	3

RYA Membership Number (For office use only)

☐☐☐☐☐☐

Instructions to your Bank or Building Society

Please pay Royal Yachting Association Direct Debits from the account detailed in
this instruction subject to the safeguards assured by The Direct Debit Guarantee.
I understand that this instruction may remain with the Royal Yachting Association
and, if so, details will be passed electronically to my Bank/Building Society.

Signature(s)

_____

Date: ☐☐ / ☐☐ / ☐☐☐☐